THE ARTS OF
DAVID LEVINE

ALSO BY DAVID LEVINE

THE FABLES OF AESOP (1975)
NO KNOWN SURVIVORS (1970)
PEN AND NEEDLES (1969)
THE MAN FROM M.AL.I.C.E. (1966)
A SUMMER SKETCHBOOK (1963)

THE ARTS OF
DAVID LEVINE

ALFRED A. KNOPF NEW YORK, 1978

THIS IS A BORZOI BOOK PUBLISHED BY ALFRED A. KNOPF, INC.

Copyright © 1978 by David Levine and Thomas S. Buechner
All rights reserved under International and Pan-American Copyright Conventions. Published in the
United States by Alfred A. Knopf, Inc., New York, and simultaneously in Canada by Random House of
Canada Limited, Toronto. Distributed by Random House, Inc., New York.
Grateful acknowledgment is made to the following for previously published material: Gambit Inc.,
New York Review of Books, and Smithsonian Institution Press.

Library of Congress Cataloging in Publication Data
Levine, David [Date]
The arts of David Levine.
Includes index.
1. Levine, David [Date]   I. Title.
NC1429.L47A4 1978   741.5'973   77-75010
ISBN 0-394-50265-5

Manufactured in the United States of America
First Edition

CONTENTS

David Levine is a major artist, a political force and a very funny person. His caricature commentaries on such subjects as the morals of Nixon (well before Watergate), Buckley's wit, the De Gaulle presence and the Kissinger style have reached out from the covers of newspapers and magazines all over the world, including *Time, Newsweek* and *Der Spiegel*. Their bite is reinforced by the hilarity of his vision—Nixon *is* funny as the Godfather—and made truly wonderful in that great Daumier sense, by some of the most glorious draughtsmanship of our time.

In art historical terms "major" means different—in our time, grossly, innovatively, obviously different; in other times the difference has been qualitative, and here is where Levine is something of an anachronism: He is better than as well as different from most of the caricaturists and figurative painters around. The full richness of the Levine difference has been obscured to a degree by a superficial resemblance to the work of others in the grand traditions of the past, a resemblance sufficient in this period of violent newness to account for the appreciation of his pictures by only the more discerning. It is time everyone took a closer look.

David Levine does two kinds of art work, and until recently they have been kept as separate as his two studios: caricature and painting. Thoroughly aware that no moment in history has ever provided such easy access to so much of the art of the past, he revels in the association with his predecessors and contemporaries through works made available by museums, dealers, collectors, books, slides and reproductions. Never consciously having to worry about developing his own style, not caring about innovation for its own sake, he continues past traditions both as caricaturist and as painter.

There are two kinds of work in this book: drawings and watercolors. The drawings done on commission and for reproduction are linear, in black and white, and are based on photographs; the watercolors done at will and for gallery sale are tonal, in color, and painted from life.

David Levine was born on December 20, 1926, in Brooklyn, New York. His father, Harry Levine, was a garment manufacturer (of ladies' dresses) and his mother, Lena, was a trained nurse. Both were politically aware and they actively participated in liberal causes, particularly the labor movement. Levine's more or less happy childhood included exposure to a good deal of social outrage and organization, of great causes to be fought for and traditional enemies to be fought against. Thus, early in his life he developed his present political orientation and, more important, his crusading spirit.

Although P.S. 241 and Erasmus High School offered some fairly stiff competition in the Brooklyn of the thirties and early forties, Levine's performance was not academically remarkable. The immense Brooklyn Museum, with its Sunday concerts, plaster casts, changing exhibitions and unkempt grounds, was more to his liking. With the goal of attaining the prerequisites for a teaching certificate in art, Levine attended and graduated from Tyler in Philadelphia. It was here that he was introduced to the theories of Dr. Albert Barnes, the Philadelphia Museum's great art collection and two lifelong friends—the art dealer Roy Davis and the artist Aaron Shikler.

Back in New York, a year with Hans Hofmann provided a close-up look at the directions modern art was taking, and an opportunity to reject them—which he did. For income, he produced cartoons, Christmas cards, book jackets and illustrations, while he continued the process of discovery begun in the Philadelphia Museum by painting pictures of family and friends. Those unique creations for which he is best known and most enjoyed—his caricatures—started with departmental headings in *Esquire* in 1958 and with full portraits in the *New York Review* in 1963. Although his paintings have sold successfully since the early 1950s (in a series of 31 one-man shows in the Davis Gallery and, later, the Forum Gallery), the endless stream of glorious caricatures is obviously an essential outlet for his expression.

He encountered his first major influence when he was about twelve. It was not one of the old masters in the Brooklyn Museum, such as Annibale Carracci (the seventeenth-century father of caricature), and had nothing whatsoever to do with social concern. It was Walt Disney. This attraction was not based on the animalization of humans (or humanization of animals); it centered on the practical business of mastering technique. He taught himself "rubberizing"—the reduction to circles of both characterization and animation. (His version of Donald Duck was irresistible and in great demand by his contemporaries.)

Almost simultaneously, the comic-book artist Will Eisner (creator of the Spirit and the Hawk)—the antithesis of Disney—became a counter-influence. This master broke up action within the cartoonist's box, used photographer's odd-angle formats and even introduced the character of a black detective. How could a garrulous duck in a sailor suit survive such competition for the interest of a teen-age Marxist? He could not, and Levine set out to learn all he could of this new hero's technique. One of Eisner's contributions was the hatched shadow (made up of closely set parallel lines) as opposed to the more usual solid black patterned shadow favored by everybody from Winslow Homer to Chester Gould (creator of Dick Tracy). Levine is a master of the hatched shadow, and the credit long given to Sir John Tenniel (illustrator of *Alice in Wonderland)* for this influence on Levine's work should probably be shared with Will Eisner.

This matter of hatching is of importance in appreciating Levine's caricatures and the influences behind them. From the Harold Foster "How-to" books, he learned curvilinear hatching and cross-hatching as an aid to developing form as well as color, texture, light and shade. George Bridgeman's anatomy books showed him how to emphasize form with minimal hatching, and from Willie Pogany's Norseman came increased respect for line subtleties and anatomical correctness.

The influence of great caricaturists of the past—Daumier, Nast, Doré, Kepler, Doyle and a great many others—can be seen not infrequently in Levine's work. Caricature itself is impossible without imitation and Levine's capacity for finding the essence of another's style is as developed as his ability to create astonishing likenesses. His first job for *Esquire* was to do a border in the style of the Richard Doyle border on the cover of *Punch.* (It should be pointed out that he is incapable of imitation in the sense of submerging his personality or style within another's in order to be mistaken for someone else; on the contrary, he parodies even those characteristics essential to recognition.)

The result of all this pragmatic study of the techniques of others has given Levine an extraordinary range of possibilities in what might seem a limited technique. Using a 2B lead pencil, he draws his caricature on two-ply rag, cold-pressed paper (no preliminary sketching), goes over it with India ink, using a metal crow quill, and finishes by erasing (with regret) the original pencil drawing. With nothing more than jet black lines, he imparts a sense of roundness, "color" (in the gray scale), the fall of light, texture (hair especially) and a striking graphic pattern, as well as a unique sense of the personality of the person being portrayed—and he does it all with great spontaneity.

David Levine has been called a romantic—for his work, not for himself. Unlike the Victorian bohemian in self-imposed exile, he has always lived in the real world and has been profoundly affected by it. Stimulated by cartoonists when in his teens, he developed his deep love and appreciation for fine artists, living and dead, when he attended Tyler, in his twenties. Aaron Shikler and Roy Davis introduced him to the aesthetic philosophy of Dr. Albert Barnes. The "transferred values" which formed the basis of Barnes's thinking were exemplified in the installation of the Barnes collection where medieval wrought-iron hinges shared the walls with paintings by Renoir and Matisse. Levine found the theory interesting but not helpful. For example, Cézanne as an orchestrator of elements is an intellectual phenomenon to be appreciated, but doesn't teach very much about handling paint. In contrast with such abstractions came the discovery of paintings by Bonnard and Vuillard—men who did with paint what only paint could do. In their pictures Levine was fascinated to see people as subjects in a primarily decorative context, to see drawing done with paint, to see pattern dominate space.

The Philadelphia Museum contained a great array of new influences vying for Levine's attention. Like Vuillard, Corot impressed him as a first-rate paint handler. He was attracted by the intimacy of the relatively small formats and the need for close inspection. Although Eakins's work was not up to scratch according to Barnes's theory, Levine was entranced by the paintings he saw. Their slablike structures built up of scientifically reasoned planes seemed curiously unmechanical and the brushwork particularly personal. All three painters—Vuillard, Corot and Eakins—have had a lasting influence on him. They were particularly sensitive to the use of grays and neutrals; they responded warmly to human beings as subjects; and each reflected his environment in his work. These qualities were shared to a lesser degree by The Eight, particularly Luks, Glackens and Sloane, whose opulent brushwork, practice of painting over dark-ground colors and choice of New York City's everyday life as subject matter were also significant influences on Levine's painting style.

Scores of major figures (and a great many minor ones) in the history of Western art have influenced David Levine in the sense that he has found qualities in their work through which he has tried to improve his own. As aware and every bit as interested as most professional art historians, he has the double advantage of enjoying the pleasures of connoisseurship while receiving practical instruction. No magpie gatherer of glittering devices, he assimilates only what can be used within his own well-understood style. He did not borrow Eakins's perspective, Corot's atmosphere or Vuillard's palette, for example, but he has found much that is useful to him in their work—and in the work of others: Pontormo's airy, beige tonality (page 15); Goya's figures' stance and solidity (page 14); Rembrandt's open darks (page 50), round heads (page 49, bottom right), old faces (page 48, bottom right); Sargent's pale complementaries (page 36); Degas's generalized color-shades (page 35); and on and on. His contemporaries also: Raphael Soyer's veneration for the old masters, his compassion for "his" people; and, most of all, Aaron Shikler's ways of generalizing, emphasis on silhouette and shared enthusiasm for painters of the nineteenth century.

For an artist with an extraordinarily personal way of seeing things, David Levine is surprisingly susceptible, if not downright receptive, to influence. And it's an ongoing characteristic; his current passion is for Japanese prints, not just for their decorative quality but for their monumentality.

From the point of view of technique, he is well described by the word he uses to characterize his own occupation: "shmearer." In oil or watercolor, charcoal, pastel or pencil (or strange combinations like pencil and oil), he works a very few elements very hard—back and forth, smearing them in and out and around until the image he has in mind begins to emerge, the deliberate inseparable from the accidental. He gradually becomes more precise but in fewer and fewer places—just enough to tell of the subject what he wishes, and not a jot more. He is the antithesis of the renderer who attempts to be a camera, to describe as much as he can of what he sees. Levine's ideas are down-to-earth, spontaneously expressed, big and up close. ("I don't believe in deep space—ten feet is plenty.")

When painting in oil, he is likely to mix up a large batch of some gray—perhaps a combination of black, white, Naples yellow and raw sienna. With straight viridian and alizarin crimson within reach, he can go green or pink with his gray. Such a range is enough to "shmear" the initial image out of an absorbent priming on rough linen canvas. ("A figure is a shaft of paint.") The paint seems to have its own life and the ability to add suggestive quality; the color range is unpredictable except that it is more limited than it appears. Precise linear strokes in viridian or cadmium orange may go on with a long-haired quill brush; or a lot of delicate work can suddenly be buried in an opaque mayonnaise of carefully mixed olive gray or black—to get back to what Levine wants to say rather than to what he sees. By the time the final glaze turns the nose even pinker, the painting time has been surprisingly short and the thinking-and-looking time very long. The palette on which much critical decision-making took place is equally surprising, because so few colors and so few mixed tones are responsible for so much richness. He is a very neat "shmearer."

In his watercolor technique, the key words are "puddle" and "wipe-out." The former might have come from Alexander Cozens (c. 1717-1786); the latter from John Sell Cotman (1782-1842)—or both from Maurice Prendergast (1859-1924). Here was perhaps the first American artist to use watercolor for his primary statement; and in flat processional patterns so different from the spacial effects traditionally achieved in this medium. Although the influence on Levine is unmistakable, he has made "puddle" and "wipe-out" his own distinctive devices. A wet puddle of diluted madder lake, its contours artfully pushed out here and there, evaporates, leaving a transparent pink area surrounded by a dense purple edge where capillary action has collected most of the pigment. It looks like an accident, provides a rich flat decorative color note and perfectly describes some essential piece of the subject. The blot created by the evaporated puddle may be over, adjacent to or involved in a "wipe-out." The ultimate in this device—return to the paper color—requires a surface that isn't stained by the watercolor pigments; a very difficult paper to find. The technique consists of reactivating dry paint in a controllable pattern with plain water and then blotting the resultant puddle with a facial tissue or sponge. This leaves a lighter shade which can be blotted and wiped to make it lighter still. A favored variant is the "wipe-out shmear" in which a more or less finished part—if not the whole subject—is lightened by rubbing with wet brush, tissue and sponge until the colors mix together to form a neutral glaze over whatever remains unactivated beneath. The whole surface can be modeled in this fashion, leaving more or less of the mixed-together paint film as desired. Even if everything is scrubbed out, pale traces remain—a gently tinted luminescence which may be essential to the quality of the finished watercolor.

Another Levine hallmark in his use of watercolor is puddling with Davys gray. This particular color dries to a chalky cool gray, the exact reverse of the warm transparent tints usually associated with watercolor—and therefore a striking foil. As a matter of fact, he often emphasizes the pale subtle results of wiping out and blotting with puddling in Davys gray—or with the heaviest, flattest opaque backgrounds he can get, applying them like masks to silhouette the subject. Black is a favorite.

In summary, Levine shmearing has the three qualities essential to his style: it's full of surprises, extremely flexible and yet impossible to fuss over without losing spontaneity.

In pen and ink – in the caricatures – technique and subject are least separable. Here the concept of the representation is usually both strong and very personal—communication takes place with utmost directness and considerable impact, obscuring the very means of accomplishment. His conceptualizing is so rich, so varied, so insightful and often so fantastic that it warrants special appreciation all by itself. Look at the Nixon series (pages 196-99): The same subject is portrayed as the Godfather, as Little Bo Peep, as Captain Queeg, as a face with a money bag nose and finally just plain. The ideas are extraordinary and they seem to flow effortlessly and endlessly from any person to be drawn: the deflated Hoover (page 185), the creating Pollock (page 63), the upping Whistler (page 62). And all this richness is achieved with lines—only solid black lines on white paper. But there are many different kinds: First is the outline like a fluid wire confining the subject, as in the portrait of De Gaulle (page 172), but sometimes used to add internal information, like Brezhnev's chins (page 173) or Frost's suspenders (page 145). Next come straight parallel lines in series—hatchings—used, as in the portrait of Proust (page 123), to add "color"—his suit and tie; *form*—the side of his nose; and shadow—under his hand. Then come hatchings which are neither straight nor parallel but which by their configuration and direction describe the form on which they lie—the side of De Kooning's nose (page 64) and under his lip, for example (these are usually used on the light rather than on the shadow side). Another kind of line is purely textural, invented to portray a particular material, usually hair;

compare Beckett (page 115), Eakins (page 57) and Dulles (page 184). The lines for wrinkles and furrows are strangely independent, wandering in and out of parallel hatchings as if they had nothing to do with each other—Thomas Eakins (page 57), for instance. As a matter of fact there are a number of lines that may be uniquely Levine's; a kind of whip that forms the ends of horizontal and diagonal hatchings is one - see Borges's forehead (page 128) or Mao's cheek (page 174). Although this linear vocabulary is impressive by itself, its use in imparting a particular aspect of the subject's personality while simultaneously developing an appropriate graphic impact is truly extraordinary. Beckett (page 115) is himself a torch, lines converging into total blacks heightening intensities of both the concept and the image.

To repeat, distinction must be made between *what* Levine draws and the *way* he draws. His subject matter and attitude arrest our attention with particular immediacy; what holds our interest—or at least mine—is his draughtsmanship. Both line and graphic shape are of a very high order—often more elegant, more subtle, more daring than the subjects themselves may warrant. He elevates through his attitude toward the art of drawing and so, in his own words, "tries to ennoble even those humans that have lost their sense of humanity."

David Levine does not feel a great distance in time from Vuillard and Eakins. Stylistically and chronologically, he isn't; art historically, he is, for a lot of "isms" have passed through the galleries in the last century. He resents being declared out of date for preferring Homer to Hofmann; he especially resents the idea that he is not of this world when it is just this world that he does care about, both politically and aesthetically. "My work represents me…and I am the present. I am a sensitized creature viewing the world and this is my statment on it" (*Time,* November 15, 1968). As might be expected, his views on the purposes of art express his own aesthetic preferences, traditional and humanist. He says he works for the applause—and criticism—of the non-art-oriented audience, as well as the cognoscenti. He defines art in terms of communication of feeling rather than relative quality, the object being to convey "an attitude toward the world for an audience of which the artist is by circumstance (not by subjective choice) aware." The key word is "attitude," for it is on the sincerity of the artist's concern for his subject that Levine makes his evaluation. Cézanne, by these criteria, is a formalist because he doesn't care about the apples he paints; while Chardin, who is drawn to objects familiar to a particular class of people, does care about his subject and so comes off better. To be genuinely important in Levinian terms, therefore, a work of art must contain evidence of the artist's concern for or with his subject; conversely, superficial involvement in the subject itself cannot in his view produce a good painting. Cézanne puts form, or the means through which content is expressed, first (as an end in itself) and so the content becomes a bore because his interest in the apples as apples is superficial and reduces the world to sameness.

To the direct question "Why are you an artist?", Levine's reply combines the ideological "I want to preach social sensitivity" with the less ambitious but not unrelated "I enjoy entertaining people." He spoke of the initial social role of the artist to amuse and to record (in his opinion, the greatest contemporary artist regardless of medium was Charlie Chaplin); and the pleasure he derives from bringing things and ideas to the attention of others (his vision of Coney Island, for example). He switched to Titian's *Christ Carrying the Cross* in the Prado as an example of profoundly poignant preaching and expressed the wish that he could paint pictures that would make people question their social responsibility. He recalled having been present in Union Square when the electrocution of the Rosenbergs as Soviet spies was announced; he described the crowd railing and a man crying and his own sense of loss. But having cited a contemporary big-point subject, he went on to say that the kind of staging and directing it would take is now the province of the film director; that he himself must concentrate on "humanism" in small scale. This is his attitude and it is profoundly sincere—toward the models in the studio, the old ladies on the beach and especially the women and men working in the garment shops. He values them; he values their work.

But he does not value contemporary presidents or prime ministers or secretaries of defense or their work. If his "simple humanism" seems a little one-sided, the implication is superficial. In this at least—and at last—he is consistent. His painted people are real; he struggles hard to give them life. His caricatured people are not; they are symbols, representing spectacular achievement or authority (some of it dangerous, in his view, and hence subject to ridicule). He once drew Adolf Hitler with no trace of exaggeration. His explanation was that you can't make

a monster out of a monster: the reality *is* the symbol. His seriousness is evident in the fact that he will not draw other people's points of view. When his work appears on the cover of *Time* or *Newsweek,* the comment the caricatures make is his own.

Indisputably and disconcertingly, David Levine is his own man. Who else would attack the bastions of capitalist materialism in the style of the illustrator of *Alice in Wonderland?* Who else would say of the contemporary international aesthetic sweeping-up from the Impressionists through all the history-making excitement of recent years: "In what has been abandoned there is great pickings." He is also very funny and being funny is important to him (and probably always has been). He reacts to tragedy with unintentional smiles and covers shyness with quipping bravado. He happily argues either side of any question and is so outrageously provocative that the most serious adversary is soon helpless with laughter. A master of mimicry—especially of himself as the eternal innocent—he loves an audience and always deserves one. Consistently paradoxical, he is also very serious. He finds nothing funny in prejudice and is himself extremely tolerant, except for those in authority. Mistrusting all establishments, especially governments, he can be depended upon to support whoever opposes them. He has the courage of his convictions and refuses even to make personally beneficial investments for fear that his money might be used to support activity which he opposes. His spirit of independence comes through a remark he once made on being Jewish: "To the degree that there is anti-Semitism in the world, I acknowledge being Jewish; in the same sense, when cartooning is ridiculed, I confess to being a cartoonist."

There was a time—and it lasted into the 1960s—when painting and caricaturing were two distinctly different arts as practiced by Levine. Painting was almost an homage to the old masters—Rembrandt-like family portraits, Eakins-like interiors, chiaroscuro panoramas of Coney Island and English-style watercolors of English-style landscapes. Caricaturing was full of cartooning, of making fun, of making a living. The interaction of these two arts has resulted in paintings that epitomize, that drive to the essence of the artist's interest in the subject before him, and in caricatures that ennoble, that suggest the draughtsmanship of Ingres rather than of Nast as the ultimate goal.

PAINTINGS

3

5

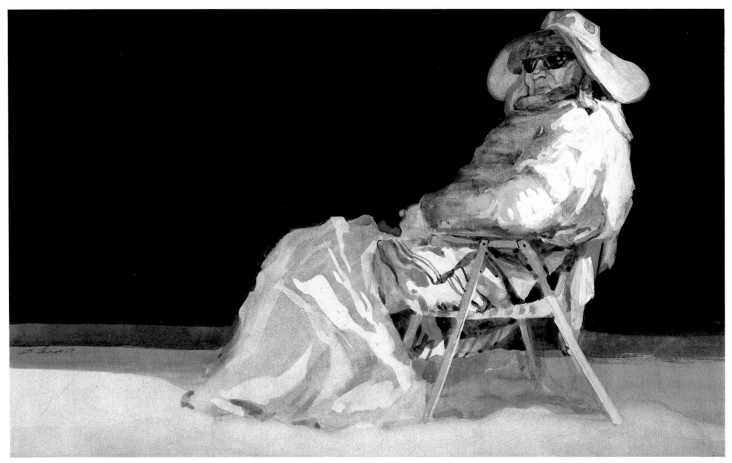

11

12

29

34

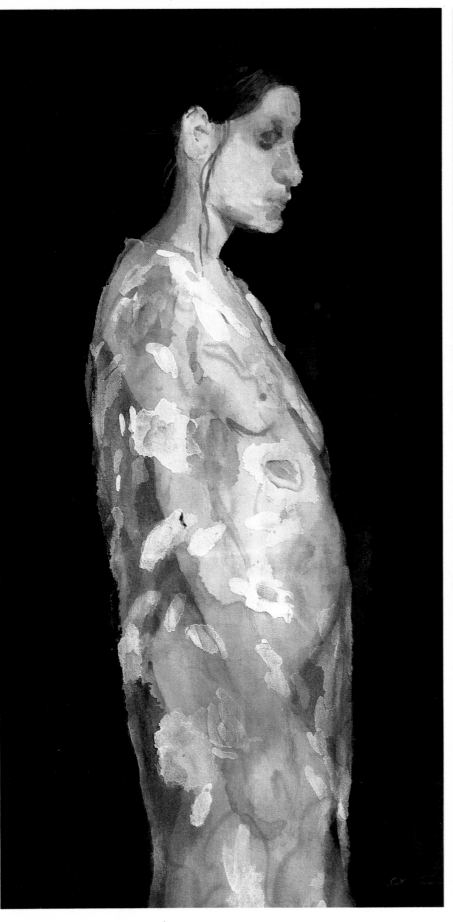

43

46

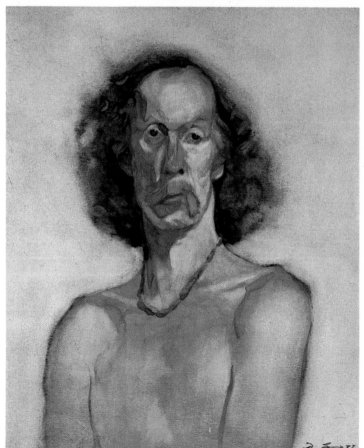

CARICATURES

LEONARDO DA VINCI

REMBRANDT VAN RIJN

TITIAN

JOHN SINGER SARGENT

THOMAS EAKINS

PAUL GAUGUIN

PABLO PICASSO

AUBREY BEARDSLEY

GEORGIA O'KEEFFE

JAMES McNEILL WHISTLER

JACKSON POLLOCK

WILLEM DE KOONING

LOUISE NEVELSON

WOLFGANG AMADEUS MOZART

FRANZ SCHUBERT

FRÉDÉRIC CHOPIN

LUDWIG VAN BEETHOVEN

RICHARD WAGNER

GIUSEPPE VERDI

HECTOR BERLIOZ

GUSTAV MAHLER

ARNOLD SCHOENBERG

JOHN CAGE

ARTHUR RUBINSTEIN

IGOR STRAVINSKY

BUSTER KEATON

CHARLIE CHAPLIN

W. C. FIELDS

WOODY ALLEN

MARILYN MONROE

BETTE DAVIS

HUMPHREY BOGART

MARLON BRANDO

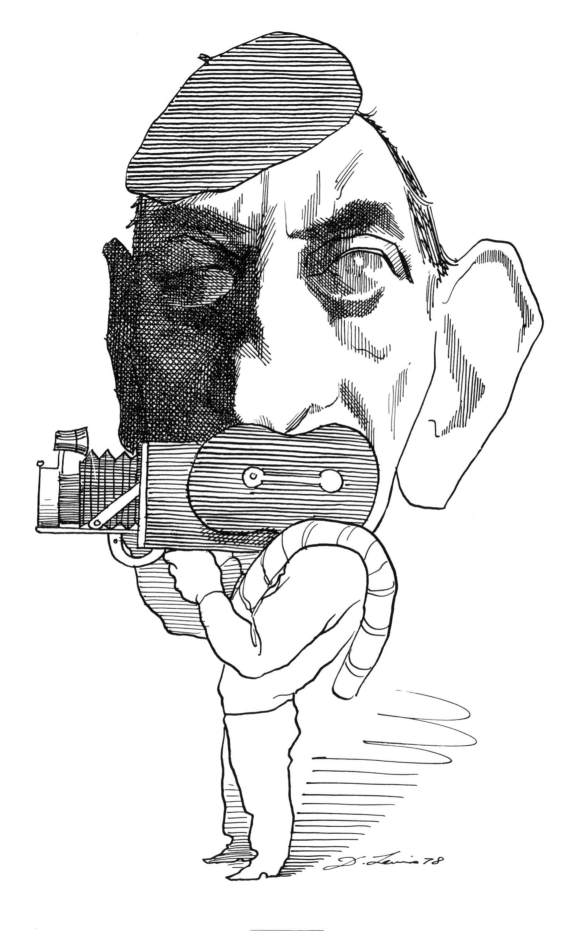

LUIS BUÑUEL

ORSON WELLES

FRANK SINATRA

LIZA MINNELLI

FRED ASTAIRE

EDITH PIAF

ELVIS PRESLEY

MUHAMMAD ALI

ISADORA DUNCAN

VASLAV NIJINSKY

WILLIAM SHAKESPEARE

JOHN MILTON

ALEXANDER POPE

SAMUEL JOHNSON

GEORGE GORDON, LORD BYRON

WILLIAM WORDSWORTH

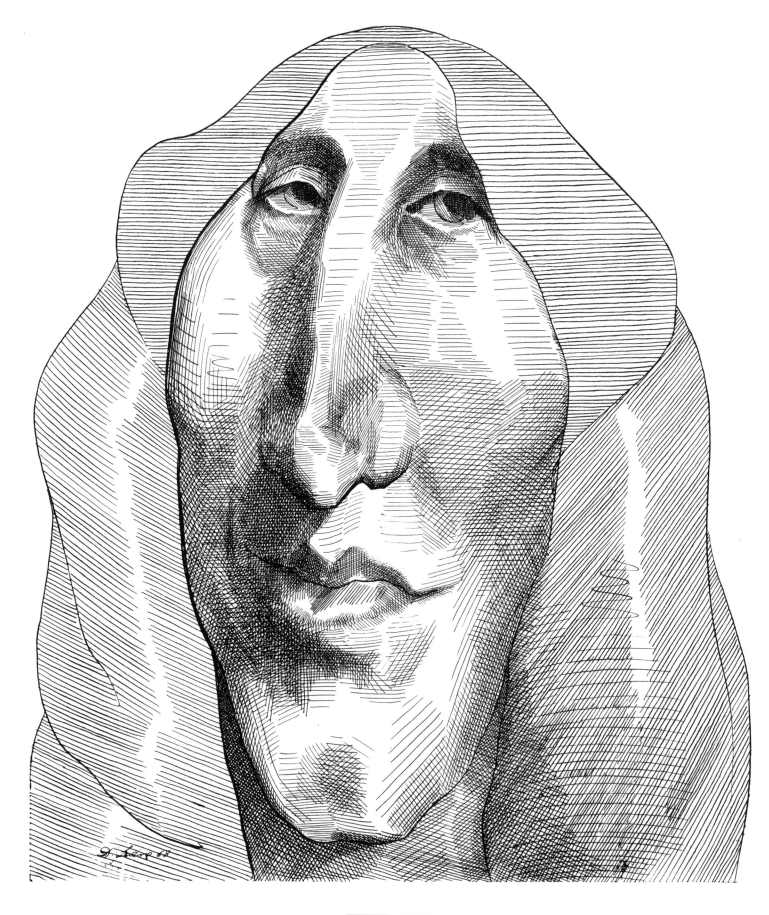

GEORGE ELIOT

OSCAR WILDE

ARNOLD BENNETT

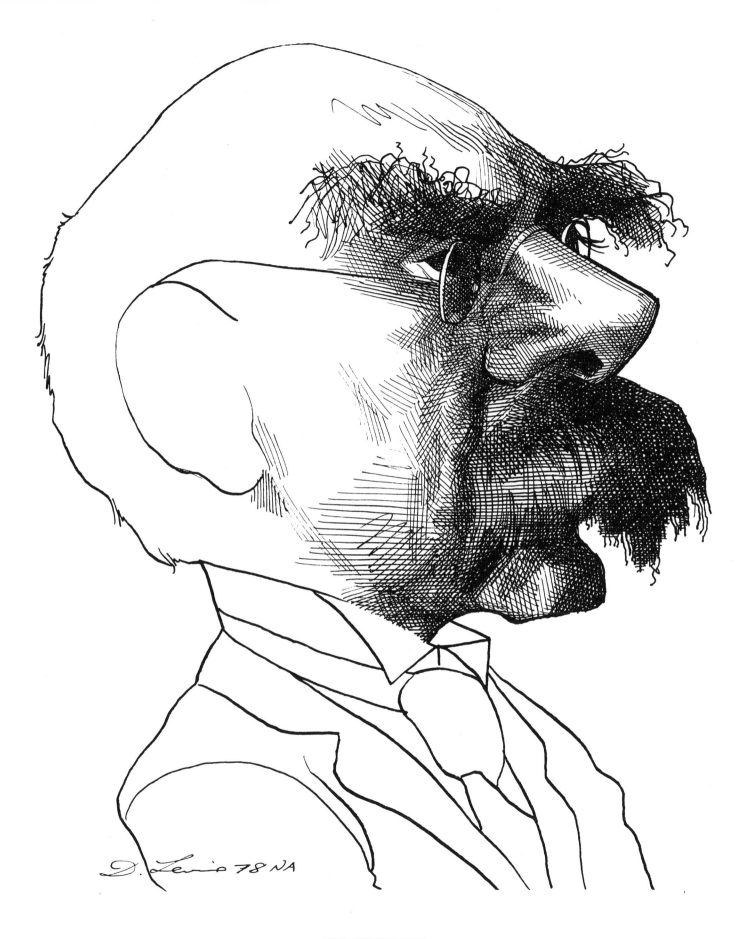

RUDYARD KIPLING

H. G. WELLS

JOSEPH CONRAD

VITA SACKVILLE-WEST

VIRGINIA WOOLF

JAMES JOYCE

ALDOUS HUXLEY

GEORGE ORWELL

DYLAN THOMAS

BERTOLT BRECHT

SAMUEL BECKETT

SIR MAX BEERBOHM

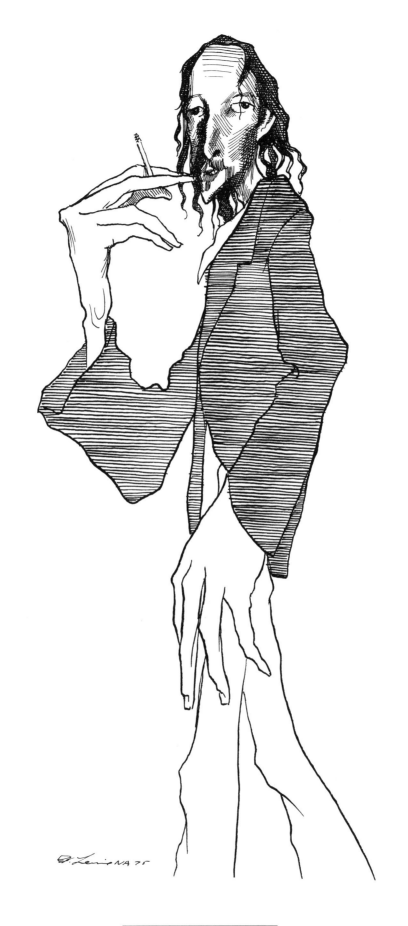

ROBERT LOUIS STEVENSON

EVELYN WAUGH

C. P. SNOW

VOLTAIRE

STENDHAL

ÉMILE ZOLA

MARCEL PROUST

COLETTE

COLETTE

JEAN-PAUL SARTRE

SIMONE DE BEAUVOIR

ISAK DINESEN

SIGMUND FREUD

ALBERT EINSTEIN

CONSTANTINE P. CAVAFY

IVAN TURGENEV

NIKOLAI GOGOL

ANTON CHEKHOV

LEV KOPELEV

NICOLAI LESKOV

ISAAK BABEL

ALEKSANDR SOLZHENITSYN

EDGAR ALLAN POE

HERMAN MELVILLE

HENRY JAMES

EDMUND WILSON

WALT WHITMAN

ROBERT FROST

GERTRUDE STEIN

ALICE B. TOKLAS

T. S. ELIOT

EZRA POUND

F. SCOTT FITZGERALD

ERNEST HEMINGWAY

151

DASHIELL HAMMETT

LILLIAN HELLMAN

SUSAN SONTAG

JOHN UPDIKE

THOMAS WOLFE

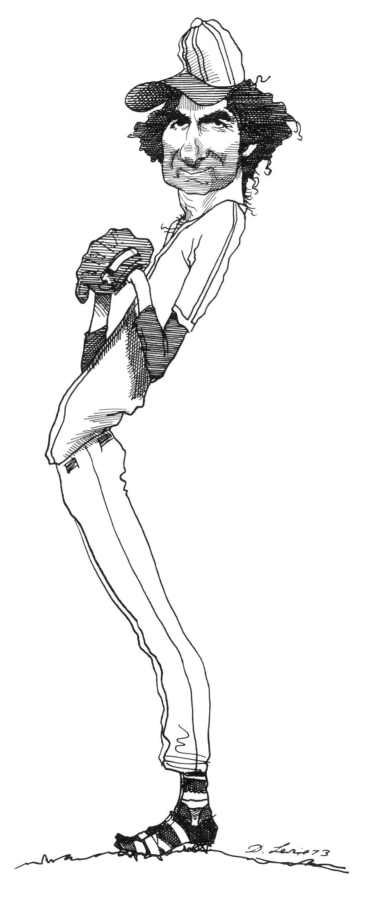

PHILIP ROTH

KURT VONNEGUT, JR.

GORE VIDAL

NORMAN MAILER

ALLEN GINSBERG

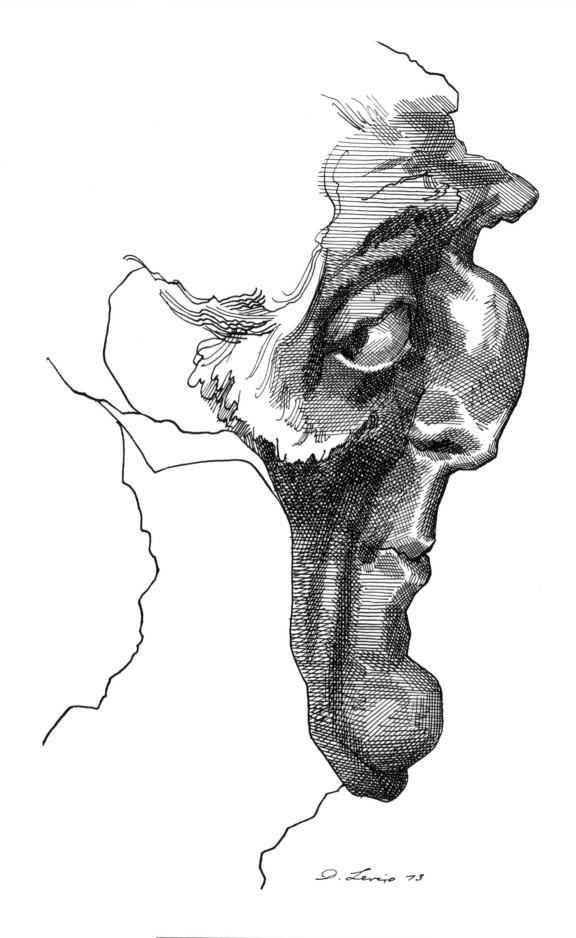

ARTHUR WELLESLEY, 1ST DUKE OF WELLINGTON

QUEEN VICTORIA

NICCOLÒ MACHIAVELLI

CRISTINA DI BELGIOJOSO

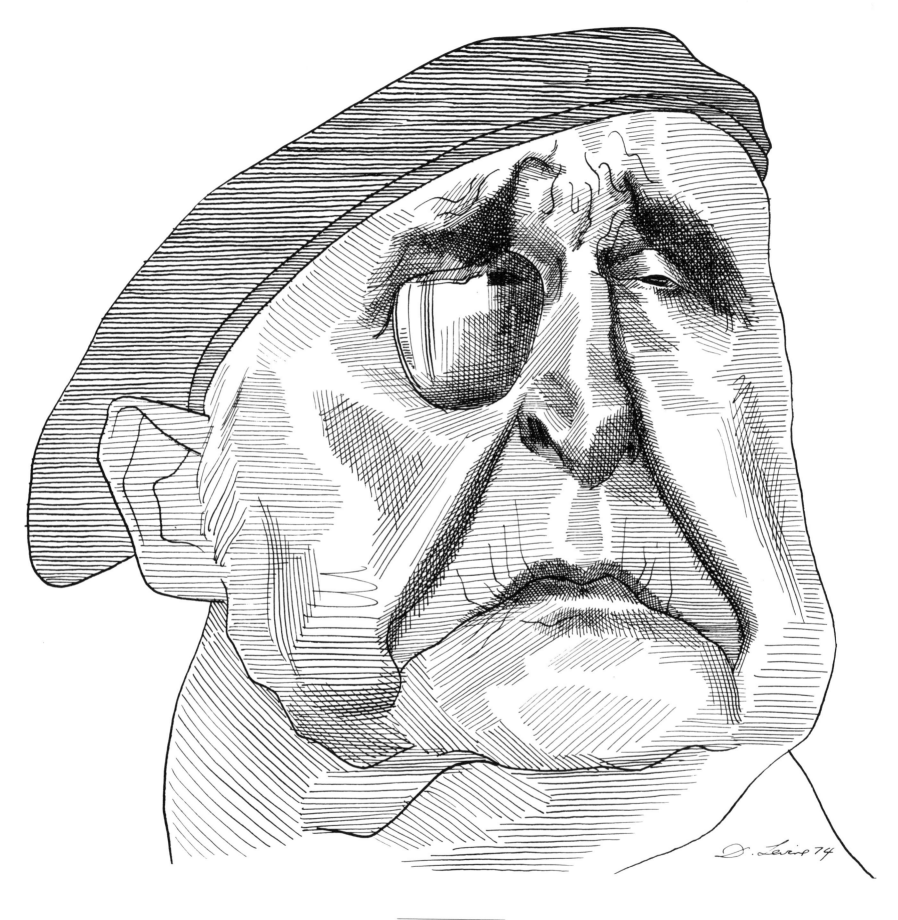

ANTONIO SPINOLA

"PAPA DOC" DUVALIER

ADOLF HITLER

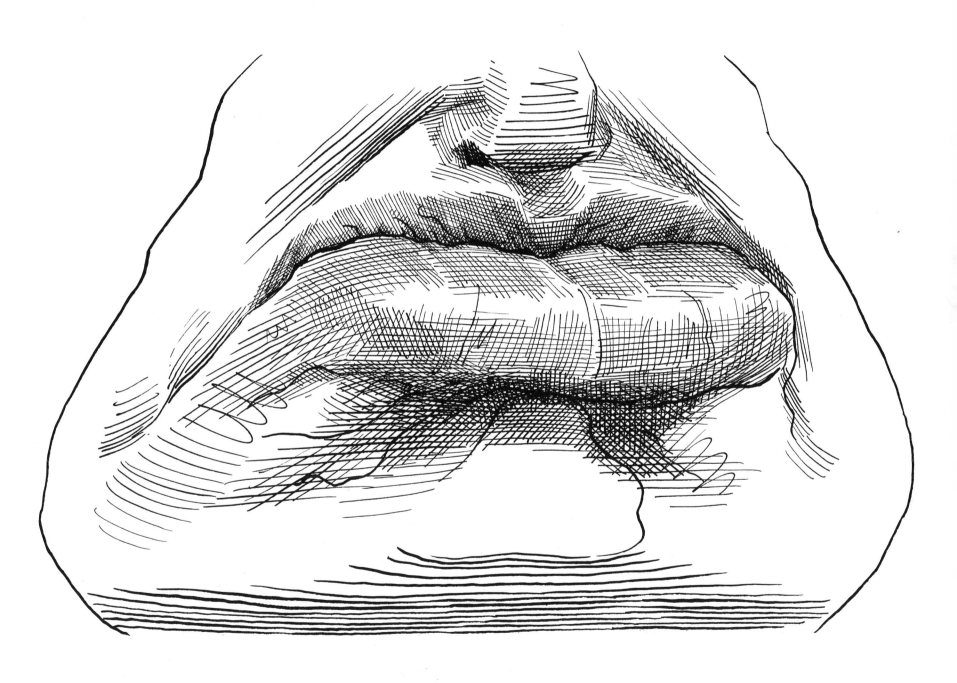

BENITO MUSSOLINI

LEON TROTSKY

JOSEPH STALIN

CHARLES DE GAULLE

LEONID BREZHNEV

MAO TSE-TUNG

CHIANG CHING-KUO

ANWAR EL-SADAT

MOSHE DAYAN

GOLDA MEIR

MENACHEM BEGIN

ELEANOR ROOSEVELT

HARRY S. TRUMAN

JOSEPH McCARTHY

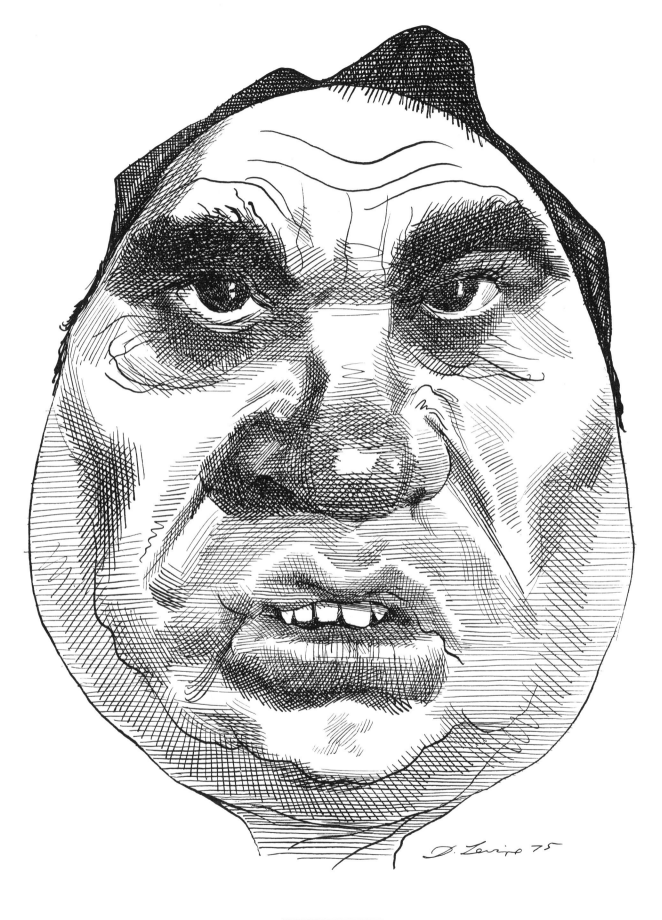

GEORGE WALLACE

JOHN FOSTER DULLES

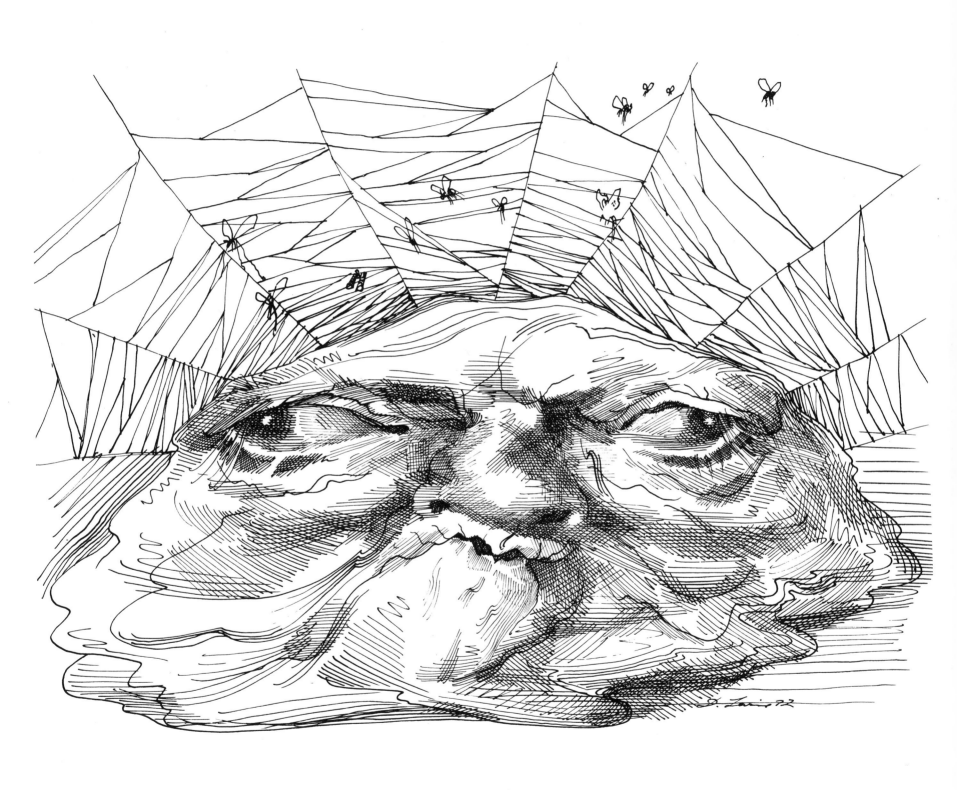

J. EDGAR HOOVER

BILLY GRAHAM

GEORGE MEANY

JOHN KENNETH GALBRAITH

WILLIAM F. BUCKLEY, JR.

EISENHOWER, KENNEDY, JOHNSON, NIXON

EISENHOWER, KENNEDY, JOHNSON, NIXON, THIEU

JOHN F. KENNEDY

EDWARD M. KENNEDY

LYNDON B. JOHNSON

HENRY KISSINGER

RICHARD M. NIXON

RICHARD M. NIXON

RICHARD M. NIXON

RICHARD M. NIXON

GERALD R. FORD

JIMMY CARTER

LIST OF PAINTINGS

INDEX OF CARICATURES

A NOTE ON THE GRAPHICS

The text of this book, as well as all the display type, was set in ITC Garamond, a modern version of the original typeface. The sixteenth-century classic Garamond design originally conceived by Claude Garamond, became one of the world's most widely used typefaces in the first half of this century. Following the American Type Founders' introduction of it to the American market in 1917, metal versions were drawn for all the typesetting machines. Tony Stan rephrased the famous Garamond flavor in twentieth-century terms for photographic and electronic typesetting machines, without deviating from the flow of line so characteristic of this distinguished letter.

This book was photo-composed on the VIP by TypoGraphics Communications, Incorporated, New York, New York. The color separations were done by Offset Separations Corporation, Milan, Italy, and New York, New York, and the four-color reproduction was done by Einson Freeman Graphics, Fair Lawn, New Jersey. The black-and-white printing was done by The Murray Printing Company, Westford, Massachussets. The book was bound by Economy Bookbinding Corporation, Kearny, New Jersey.

Ellen McNeilly directed the production and manufacturing.
Sara Eisenman assisted in the design and layout.
Lidia Ferrara art directed and designed the book.